Foreword

There's so much love in the world; but it's seldom shown,

only few can testify to it's existence..

Acknowledgement

A big thanks to my family, friends and fans. Your motivating words is what keeps my ink flowing.

The Love Charmer

Is the feeling of love inappropriate?

Is caressing our tender skin unsuitable?

Our rising heat we were made to infiltrate,

As our burning passion went unstable.

Now I'm seized by you,

I think of nothing else but you,

When I look at another, I see only you.

I don't know if this feelings are true,

Because everything you request I do.

You've made my mind to clutter,

Have you gotten what you're after?

Or have you gotten another reason?

Because together we are in this prison.

Well, for now I've got nothing to say,

I'll have to wait for another day,

I'm astonished you got me unaware,

For I perceive your spells everywhere.

But know that once this spell depreciate,

We will dance to the tune of fate

For whatever that is meant to be,

For sure, will eventually be.

Now decide your choice with wiseness,

For only but one chance you've got with me,

For if you decide to play with cleverness,

Dancing on your woes will be of me.

Now gaze into your cauldron of spells,

And tell me of what it smells,

Is this what you wish to perceive?

Or is it me you want to deceive?

You was awake all night

Meditating without respite,

Strengthening your spells with might,

Never letting the sparrow out of your sight,

Waiting for the portion to strengthen overnight.

Be mindful when you look upon me

With burning desire and lust,

Put not all hope on me;

For I arise when you think I am lost.

For if you force me to love you

With your own bloody spell,

Then my love I'll grant you

But I must say it won't finish well.

For like a tiger in the jungle,

Some hearts I've torn apart.

For it all starts with a rumble,

Making my emotions to depart.

Each one just like you,

For they all have no clue

That no one tells me what to do.

For if you can't entice my love for you

Without making the inclusion of a spell,

Then my first move of kiss to you

Will make your soul burn like hell.

So with your spells and portion you can go,

With caution you should use it if you must,

But know that any love that comes with it so

Will be without dignity and trust.

And for sure they will seem to love you,

And they will be your puppet,

You'll get bored and loosen your glue

But this play they won't ever forget.

How can you be free of this?

You have only two choices;

Is either you murder them,

Or you get murdered by them.

So preserve yourself from the heart attack,

Or better be like me without a slack,

For like a tiger in the jungle

Each I freed by slaying them without fumble.

Will You?

Will you stand firm with me?

When the storm comes raging,

The sun starts scorching,

The wind starts blazing,

The rain comes flooding,

The moon starts fading…

Will I be consoled by you?

When the eyes starts weeping,

The heart starts breaking,

The mind starts cluttering…

Will you still be by me?

When the skin starts itching,

The head starts aching,

The legs starts giving way,

The hands starts shaking…

Will you still hold on to this love?

When my mood starts swinging,

Anxiety comes peeping,

Trouble comes knocking,

Torment comes visiting,

Sorrow comes sitting,

And tragedy comes striking…

Will you??

©Saint GozKa'EL

This Rollercoaster

* * *

When we first met, I thought I understood love,

I thought I know all its move;

All its problems I had confidence I could solve,

And its worth I believed I can prove,

But I wasn't correct about this comprehension!

As you allowed me into your heart,

Feelings I never knew engulfed my every part,

My everyday thought by you was hazed,

Into your eyes I couldn't help but gazed.

You filled me with bountiful pleasures,

You became the most precious among my treasures;

We were together like ice and fire,

And you filled my days with blissful desire!

Those desires were like portals

Leading to a world of wondrous love of immortals

Where our soul, our love, and our heart

Could be bonded together and never apart.

I was made to learn how to clean up my stains,

To stand strong and brave in pains,

To love myself against all hates,

All these you taught me as soulmates.

Your love lights up my path,

A strong beating for you is done by my heart,

As I sleep and wake up to the morning dew

I bless daily that day which I met you.

No matter what the case may be,

No matter where life may tilt us,

On this love's path with you I'll always be

And our hearts will be warmth with love so marvelous

©Saint GozKa'EL

Of that which supposed to occur,

Of that which once occurred,

Of that which is occurring,

And of that which will occur.

All of one, Four things in diverse;

A loving soul,

A loyal spirit,

A craving mind,

And a pure heart of love.

Four times death have knocked:

First time my eyes beheld you,

First time you looked into my eyes,

First time I felt your skin and we kissed,

And first time you departed from me.

Four times I have frozen:

I was enchanted by your beauty,

Your smile captivated my heart,

Your kiss froze me on a spot,

And your touch made my head to go light.

But two things I will promise;

No matter where you may be,

My love for you will always forever be.

Sad Text From My Love Notes

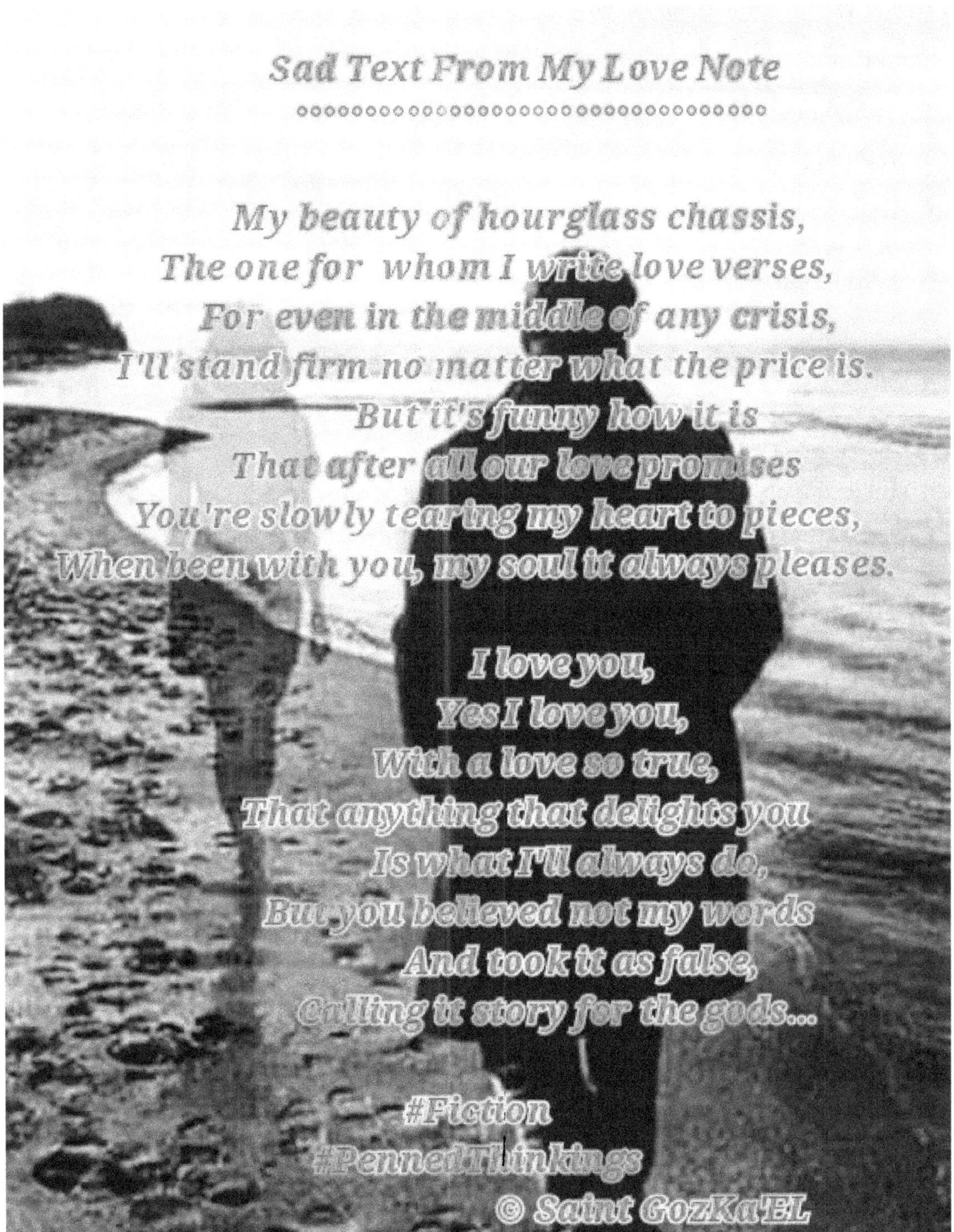
Sad Text From My Love Note
My beauty of hourglass chassis,
The one for whom I write love verses,
For even in the middle of any crisis,
I'll stand firm no matter what the price is.
But it's funny how it is
That after all our love promises
You're slowly tearing my heart to pieces,
When been with you, my soul it always pleases.
I love you,
Yes I love you,
With a love so true,
That anything that delights you
Is what I'll always do,
But you believed not my words
And took it as false,
Calling it story for the gods...
#Fiction
#PennedThinkings
© Saint GozKa'EL

My beauty of hourglass chassis,

The one for whom I write love verses,

For even in the middle of any crisis,

I'll stand firm no matter what the price is.

But it's funny how it is

That after all our love promises

You're slowly tearing my heart to pieces,

When been with you, my soul it always pleases.

I love you,

Yes I love you,

With a love so true,

That anything that delights you

Is what I'll always do,

But you believed not my words

And took it as false,

Calling it story for the god…

© Saint GozKa'EL

I've got no plan

To play with your heart,

for nothing I'll stand to gain,

I've got no plan to break it apart,

Neither will I cause you pain.

I ain't planning to leave you alone

For we've got a deal,

I know I'm bad at calling on phone,

A warm love from me I want you to feel.

I've got no games to play ,

Ain't brutal and unkind,

Not gonna torment you any day,

Never gonna mess with your mind.

My love I'm gonna prove to you,

Once and for all

When the time is due,

For you won't regret this love you fall.

Am never gonna play with your heart,

Never gonna leave you behind,

Never gonna tear your heart apart,

Never gonna mess with your mind.

Let's make a love that will not die,

Lets make memories without a sad cry,

Let's roll with our hearts in a love knot-tie,

Let's make this bliss not to go askew,

Let's bring this love into light so true…

© Saint GozKa'EL

As we penetrate deep into each other's thinking,

Inside of us, warm feelings began to grow,

As into the ocean of love we began sinking,

For us, heartfelt affections we began to show.

I just know that infatuation is not what we feel,

Inside our hearts, the feeling of love is so real,

As our spirits feel the same power, our minds have become weak,

We no longer dwell on thoughts, for it's our feelings that now speak.

Do not be surprised how we came to be,

For the universe is in support of us,

For they conspired with me,

To bond the two of us.

Only our heart's beating now have every word to say,

As we're bent on not breaking away,

For every love's price we're ready to pay,

As together we're forever gonna stay!

©Saint GozKa'EL

Sweet-scented lies so decoying,

Elegant hour-glass figure so captivating,

Smooth lustrous hair so silky,

Bright sparkling eyes so spellbinding.

Rich luscious lips so appealing,

Luxuriant lithe laps so alluring,

Spine-weakening touches so arousing,

The nectar of your lips sweeter than sugar,

Yet more poisonous than the venom of a black mamba.

You're such an enchanting Delilah!

So wilful in your games,

So cunning with your colourful charms.

Braced with a soft sultry voice ,

With which she puts men of valor

To slumber upon her bosom.

I wonder how our paths crossed,

And with ourselves we got engrossed.

She's a queen-game-planner,

I'm a king-game-maker.

We only passed by to play on ourselves a little trick,

Now we've gotten sick

And we're now trapped in this trip.

She's kneading her plans in her dark mind,

Working with her dark essence to make me go love-blind.

Oh sweet lovely Delilah

Don't take me for a fool

Just because I'm keeping my cool,

For I can lure you into Love's pool

And watch as you drown and drool.

Now you see what you did to yourself?

Your dilemma just keep piling,

And what did I do to myself?

I just keep smiling!

As the nights gets scary,

And the stars starts disappearing,

And the moon starts dimming,

And the sky starts darkening,

Forget not, I'll be with you….

As the storms comes raging,

And fierce winds comes blowing,

And hopes starts thinning,

And faith starts shaking,

Forget not, I'll stand by you…

By you, no loosing of a tear

You'll have no cause for a fear,

Your faith and hope must be stronger,

In all frivolity, you must stand bolder,

Forget not, I'll be there …

In loses and dispiriting,

Helpless and discouraged,

Disappointment and heartbreaks,

You won't ever bear alone,

You must forget not, I'll be by your side….

As your smiles turns to joyful laughter,

Your happiness to passionate affection,

And your giggles to gleeful bliss,

Forget not, I'll got your back…..

You're my reason for surviving,

My true source of joy,

My priceless jewel,

My ocean of gleeful bliss

My never-ending sea of passionate affection...

Forget not, I'm he whose love you'll uphold

Forget not, I'm he whose touch fills your

stomach with butterflies,

I'm the one whose kiss sends shivers

down your spine,

Getting your life filled with sweet

smiles and lovely memories....

Forget not, by me you're

cherished beyond words!.....

©Saint GozKa'EL

The memories of you I can't erase,

Cos we went through a phase,

Even if I simply unfriend you,

I know I still can't forget you.

It's quite unfortunate of the relationship,

Now I know not all things speed like a bullet,

Some sail steadily like a cargo ship.

I just hope we aren't less valued than a mullet.

In my mind, your pictures I can't take back,

The sound of your beautiful laughs I can't delete,

And the frames of your beautiful smiles just got stack,

If those memories of us is what I can delete

I would have gladly done it.

But alas!, those memories are stuck there,

Etched in my mind, I still know of it,

Instilled in my being here,

Grasping on to me,

Those unending memories of our past

Are been forced to be ignored by me...

Some days when they flood back in vast

My eyes I force to close...

As they run through me...

I just breath deep through my nose

Those memories of you and me

I just hope with time I will forget,

But sometimes I wished we never met...

©*Saint GozKa'EL*

I knew I loved you,

And it was a love so true,

For that love to be reciprocated by you,

Is something I wished too.

This love I have for you

Is so wide like the ocean,

And whenever am with you

I feel so comfortable like on a cushion.

This feeling wasn't from the start,

But it suddenly formed like a cast,

And I opened up to you from my heart,

And I wished your own euphoria will start.

My level of love for you was so high

That no one could ever attain,

I was drawn to you with a strong tie

And hoped my love your heart will contain.

I opened up to you that I love you

I think there's no need to lie,

But I have no clue

That you won't allow us to give it a try.

To you I opened my heart

That I got a love so real,

And I wished from the start

That you'll also have this love to feel.

All you did was to tell me

Was That this love which I confess to you,

Is something you can't reciprocate to me

Even as little as a drop of dew.

And The love which you got for me

Only stopped at friendship level,

That you'll keep this friendship with me

And never allow it to be broken like a gravel.

©Saint GozKa'EL

The Love I Craves

Dear sweet lover,

You're the apple of my eyes,

And I want you to realize,

That so long this love hardens like ice,

Your soul I'll never slice,

For this love I'll always be nice.

Whoever hurts you I'll paralyze,

My heart will throb for you till the day the sun stops to rise.

Quench my thirst

With the wine

Of your rugged love,

And let me have a taste

Of the sweet delicacy

Of your undying sin.

Don't just forget;

You've got that special thing,

I'll never trade you for anything.

You're comparable to nothing.

So long the clock keeps ticking,

My love for you will keep kicking.

Get me tipsy with the vinegar

From your venomous lips,

As you burns through my skin

With your unabating desire.

As I set my gaze on your groovy smile,

Let me get consumed

By your Passion's ardent furnace,

While we slowly gets projected

Into the endless world

Of passionate affection.

© **_Saint GozKa'EL_**

As I gaze into your eyes,

With eyes full of adoration,

Your beauty makes my

heart freezes just like ice.

Your sweet sultry kiss,

Sends shivers down my spine.

Feel safe, this love won't go amiss,

For forever will I protect you as mine.

As I softly caress your hair

While we're cuddled, breathing romance into the air,

Continually will I make you feel loved.

To you my sweet Queen,

The beauty that my eyes

behold on a steady,

The one that gives me joy in the morning,

And makes me smile in the evening

Do I forever belong to…

Love's Trial of Hope

I thought being funny will make you fall for me,

But how the table turned to me is now funny,

For just a beauteous smile from you

Makes me fall more in love with you.

The joy your lovely giggles gives me

I do wonder how it came to be.

Me and you, living the best of our lives,

And breezing through many lovely moments,

Is one of the wishes for which I craves.

A hope worth promising for the future days.

Till that day comes,

I'm left with no other choice,

Than to take delight

In the beautiful twinkle

Of your sparkling eyes.

I'll always smile at your gleeful laughter,

And above all, you shall be embraced

With every ounce of my mind, soul and heart.

Bear this in mind;

On the steps to forever,

There you'll always find me,

With endless love, Calmly waiting for you,

For you're my lady of a special kind.

©*Saint GozKa'EL*

A Guiltless Kiss

I heard as you gave a painful hiss,

When you saw me kiss an innocent kiss.

I never wished for it to come to that,

Am sorry it hit you like an assassin's dart.

That kiss you saw me kiss,

Is just an innocent kiss;

My heart was purely plain,

I never knew it will put you in pain.

For the kiss, that I've already kissed,

And now I know, with me you're pissed.

Pardon me for that my misdeed,

For with you I'm been candid:

For that which you saw me did,

Was done with the pure heart of a kid.

With me you've stopped talking,

Now away should I start walking?

With you, I think I've pleaded much,

It hurts me that you take it as such;

For my sins, I'm ready to pay,

What have you got to say?

You see that person you saw me kissed?

We have nothing to do with each other,

It's only her partner that she missed,

And they both really loves each other.

If that my action really hurt you,

Then any punishment I'll accept in full due,

I promise never again to try that,

For my heart will never allow us to go apart.

© *Saint GozKa'EL*

Mumbling Heart

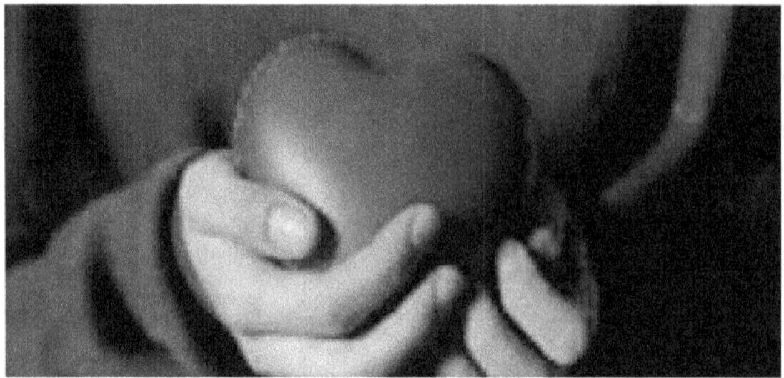

All the sweet raw kisses,

We once shared in different pieces,

Are still hot in my mind like an amber,

And as you gave me all you had,

Those sweet memories I still remember.

As in all truthfulness I'm clad,

To tell you that whilst I stands,

To you i stretch forth my hands

To offer you all that's left of me,

For with you is all my soul craves to be.

Here I sit reminiscing,

On the moments I spent with you,

And I found myself missing,

Every bit of my time with you.

While in this reverie of mine,

I penned a thousand love notes;

When my heart still can't feel fine

I ripped them to bits like clothes.

I shed a bucketful of tears,

In the dark, they dried up against my fears.

I wondered within myself,

How again will I feel your tender touch?

So I dipped my hand inside my heart's crouch

And stands to give you every part of mine self.

© ***Saint GozKa'EL***

Love's Twists

I'm not afraid to thread on the path of love;

But the thought of its loss makes me pray for a curve.

I do not think much of love's price;

But its cost makes me think twice.

For its players, I have nothing to worry about;

But its game is fiercer than a wresting bout.

I can easily adapt to its rules;

But its name have turned some men into fools.

For Love's grasp, I have no fear;

But its hold I know can cause a tear.

Love's fire can be made light by a gentle breeze;

But Love's cold? It won't take long to make you freeze!.

Hunger for love can be overcomed;

But thirst for it is hard to be abandoned.

Love's beauty is ever pleasing to the soul and eyes;

But its curse can be freezing to the heart like ice.

©Saint GozKa'EL

As I stands

Why am I so much engulfed with the thoughts of you?

It's more than just your beauty, or what say of you?

Is it your adorable smiles?

Or your beautiful laughs that sends me across miles?

The way you have effects on me I just can't explain,

Your lovely giggles, so beautifully plain,

The cute twinkles in your eyes captivates my heart,

So amazing is your charm, personality, soul and heart.

I know there's many reasons why I'm enchanted by you,

And that keeps me wishing as time flew,

To spend the larger part of my days with you,

For if this wish of mine can become true,

In countless ways not so few,

I'll show you the amazing blessing you're to me.

How much you mean to me, you have no clue,

For you're so much appreciated by the whole of me.

By your cute smile, my attention is held,

Your charming muses gets me nailed,

The way you talks, my mind is captured,

By your lovely laughter, my heart is captivated,

When into my eyes you looked,

Forever my love you won.

As my heart as one is still panting,

You should bear in mind that I'm still standing.

© *Saint GozKa'EL*

This Pain!

The pain of holding unto someone who have shown you their back,

The pain of building a bridge that have been broken,

The pain of lighting a flame that have lost it's spark,

The pain of clinging to a love that have left without a token.

Haven't you felt This pain?!

The pain of putting together a heart that have been shattered,

The pain of picking broken parts that have been battered,

The pain of reviving a chocolatebunny

That melted cos the day was hotly sunny.

The pain of been so sad even when friends try to sound funny,

The pain of losing thoughts, cos against you, your whole being now acts cunny.

Oh This pain!!

The pain of trying to trash memories which got stuck in your head,

The pain of trying to revive feelings which have only gone dead,

The pain of holding unto promises which was made on the bed,

The pain of 'never letting go' just as a lover once said.

Yes, this pain!!

The pain of your soul longing to merge again,

The pain of your body trying to clear out the stain,

The pain of your mind saying 'give it a try once again'.

The pain of your lover not giving you a chance

To bring your self out of your trance,

And try to make things to be back on balance!.

Sometimes I stagger in daylight,

Like I'm drunk with wine,

Many demons to fight,

But I keep posing like I'm fine.

Walk with me in the dead of the night,

Hold me tight when I'm in fright,

When I'm flawed, make me feel alright,

When my demons rises, stand with me to fight,

Embrace me affectionately. I won't be out of your sight.

While in the front line,

I'm placed like a false nine

But I've got to be scoring like a top nine.

Getting along, putting depression on the punchline,

Jumping loops, escaping spirits with whom I dine,

Making a hardbite, with a strong built canine.

Walk with me in the dead of the night,

Hold me tight when I'm in fright,

When I'm flawed, make me feel alright,

When my demons rises, stand with me to fight,

Embrace me affectionately. I won't be out of your sight.

Got to do some storing up, for any impending famine,

Claiming fake love, it's me you want to whine?

Take life's chaos as a good sign,

For when destiny and future will align

This love together we will define and refine.

Walk with me in the dead of the night,

Hold me tight when I'm in fright,

When I'm flawed, make me feel alright,

When my demons rises, stand with me to fight,

Embrace me affectionately. I won't be out of your sight.

Fantasy Bliss

I kept her in wait

While she was wet,

She got a confident gait,

And she wasn't easy to get.

I meant no harm

Love was my only charm,

She's the sweetest rose in my farm

And I can't let her out of my palm.

My shoulders I lowered down,

And made her to calm down,

That I only went down town,

So no much need for a frown.

The words I got are few,

For how much I love you

You got no clue,

And this love I'll prove to you

When the time is due.

© Saint GozKa'EL

My True Confidence,

In you I've found a sure providence,

As I'm in no doubt about your prudence,

I place my heart to you as a pure evidence.

It wasn't my plan to meet you

But the universe conspired with me

And brought you

To me.

The first time I set my eyes on you

I was awe-struck,

When I tried speaking to you

Words in my throat got stuck.

You've got a beauty so rare,

To none I can't compare.

You're so gorgeously endowed,

Only you my eyes have always adored.

Take a look into my eyes,

And see through my heart.

Let me be your fire and you be my ice,

And let's build love that won't tear apart.

For the words I got are few,

Am sure you have no clue,

How much am captivated by you,

For my words of love I'll prove to you,

When the time is due…

I've rounded the world's circumference,

And I found none like you,

I place my heart as a sure evidence

You surely is my true confidence.

©Saint GozKa'EL

My Crush

From a distance I've always admired you;

Cos from a distance, I'm shielded away from pain.

In my dreams I've loved you;

Cos in my dreams, there's no rejection.

You have become my everyday thought,

For I can't get you off my mind.

If true love could be bought,

I'll buy you for you're one of a kind.

For your beauteous glow, the stars can't match;

For your elegance, the moon can't withstand.

When you smile, the sun stands in awe to watch,

The way you create butterflies in my stomach, I still don't understand.

If you'll grant me a chance to love you,

I promise never to hurt you,

I'll cherish you with everything within my power,

And I'll keep you from harm in my safety tower.

I'll build you an empire,

And you will be the super queen of my kingdom,

My love for you will never expire,

For we shall ride in love with wisdom.

As my love, I'll take you to the moon ;

There we shall embrace in a warm romance,

My words of love I'll prove to you soon,

If allowed, I promise you'll never regret this chance.

With unending compassion, your heart will be filled;

With undying love, your soul will be filled.

All these I'll bring to reality,

If only you turn my fantasy to reality,

By giving me a chance to make you my lover,

And we shall sail on this love voyage forever.

©*Saint GozKa'EL*

Most times I'm lively,

And to you I'll look lovely,

Just cherish me instantly

Because I can change momentarily.

Please be distressed less

For my mood easily get changed,

As my demons gets me caged,

They throng in and get my mind barraged,

And my mood level I can't get gauged.

It causes me feeling of sadness,

It elevates my thinkings of gloom,

Into thin air vanishes my gladness,

Even as I abhor the thoughts of doom.

Still, Nevertheless;

This bad mood of mine wears out soon,

While in some cases it lasts a longer time,

As my mind gets anguished with a bad tune,

The demons causes in my mind a foggy clime.

So my sweet Empress

When I thrusts you off

Just as most times I do,

Don't have the thoughts of

That I don't want to be with you.

Sometimes when my mood swings,

Far off from me I'll want you to be.

But to understanding I wish you clings,

That through me I want you to see.

I want you to be fearless

Far off from me I never wanted you,

For what I'm trying to say

Is 'Please pull me closer to you'

And leave me not and go far away.

Stronger is what your love gets me,

Better closer as can be I want you near me.

When my mood swings over me,

In your arms you have to take me,

Closer to you, you have to pull me,

And there you'll get to understand me

That with you all I want is to see me.

©Saint GozKa'EL

This is said to be the month of romance,

When love is given a huge chance,

To show to one another

That they're the best like no other.

As I wallow in my world of fantasy,

Wishing my wishes will become real

For you to read deep into my poetry

And understand how you make me feel.

Thoughts of you have beclouded my mind,

My lady, you're just one of a kind.

You got a beauty so divine,

My desire is to make you my valentine.

I will amaze you with lovely-scented flowers,

And sweet-tasting chocolates,

I'll prove my love and make it rain on you like warm showers,

For been with you is all my heart craves.

Can this wishful fantasy of mine ever become real?

Is there any chance that I'll ever get to make you mine?

For with a heart full of love before you I've come to kneel,

Asking you to be my forever valentine.

©Saint GozKa'EL